L is for Love

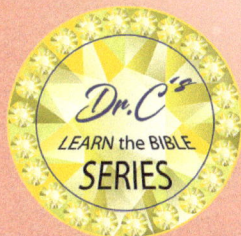

Dr. C. White-Elliott
Illustrated by Ariel

www.clfpublishing.org
909.315.3161

Cover design by Senir Design.

Contact info: info@senirdesign.com

Illustrated by Ariel.

ISBN #978-1-945102-65-3
Printed in the United States of America.

Dedicated to the White Family:

Aaron, Sr.

Jeri

Kimara- 10 yrs.

Aaron, Jr.- 9 yrs.

Aaron II- 8 yrs.

Kayden- 4 yrs.

Kingston- 3 yrs.

Zuri- 3 months

1 Corinthians 13:13 (NIV): *"And now these three remain: faith, hope and love. But the greatest of these is love."*

The greatest love story ever told is the one found in the Holy Bible, telling us in John 3:16, *"For God so loved the world that he gave his one and only Son, that whoever believes in him shall not perish but have eternal life."*

When we look around, we can see love all around us.

In a land, not so far away, lives a happy family. In the family are Daddy, Mommy, and their six children: Kimara, Junior, Papi, Kayden, King, and Baby Zuri.

In this family, there is a lot of love, and it can be seen in everything they do and in all the fun they have together.

On warm days, the family goes into the backyard for a cookout. Daddy makes hotdogs and hamburgers on the grill for the children, while Mommy sits by the swimming pool, as the children splash and play.

On cold days, Mommy warms the children's tummies with hot chocolate and marshmallows. Look, Kayden has chocolate on her nose!

For birthdays, there is always a big
birthday party with a jumper, a birthday
cake, beautiful decorations, and a pinata.
Look at all the candy falling out!

At dinner time, everyone wants something different to eat. Kayden and King love chicken nuggets. Kimara, Junior, and Papi love hot wings. So, Mommy makes everyone's favorite food.

But, what about the baby? She is too young
to eat what everyone else eats, so Daddy
gives Zuri a bottle before she goes to sleep.
That feels good to her tummy.

In the evenings, after all the kids take their baths and go to bed, Daddy and Mommy have some quiet time to themselves. They enjoy an ice cream cone, a popsicle, and a good movie.

Families all over the world are filled with love. Take a look around your home. How much love do you see being shared by your family?

www.ingramcontent.com/pod-product-compliance
Lightning Source LLC
Chambersburg PA
CBHW041957100426
42813CB00019B/2910